T5-AFD-240

THOUGHTS

On relationships

by

Paul Liebau

Illustrations by Barry Trower

P.S.A. Ventures
London, Canada

Copyright © 1985 by Paul Liebau
For permission to use the thoughts
or illustrations in this book,
contact the author c/o the publisher.

The author sincerely invites you to

send him your reactions and reflections.

Mail to:

P.S.A. Ventures
92 Susan Ave.
London, Ontario
Canada N5V2G4

First Printing   April 1985   2,000 copies
Second Printing   October 1985   5,000 copies

ISBN 0-9691999-0-2

Printed in Canada

Dedicated

to my children, Sharon and Ann
whose presence I appreciate
whose courage amaze me, and
whose psychological growth
is an inspiration to me.

AUTHOR'S NOTE

I began writing this book in France in March, 1984 very early in the last morning of a delightful visit with my daughter Ann.

THOUGHTS, like these, emerge over time and experience, and most pages were written while travelling in England, Hong Kong, the Philippines, Japan, California, British Columbia and the Yukon.

I feel tremendous excitement sharing them with you.

Paul Liebau

A

Potential

Friend

Is

Only

A

"Hello"

Away

IF

YOU EXPECT ME

TO BELIEVE YOU

THEN

TELL ME THE TRUTH

noone else
can
make you
happy

YOU
have to do that
for yourself

If I

hide

something

from you

I

give you reason

not to trust me

11

Please

don't ever
give me

a sugar-coated
poison pill

Fear

can keep us from

even dreaming

DARE TO DREAM

There is no

"right"

way

We each

have to

figure out

our own "right" way

To

love

is to set

ourselves and others

FREE

TOO OFTEN

PARENTS

PROTECT CHILDREN

FROM TRUTH

WHAT REALLY HURTS

IS

THE <u>NOT KNOWING</u>

Be careful

What you want

you'll

probably

get it

The person
we hang onto

we push   away

There
are
no

accidents

People

require

their _own_ power

to assume responsibility

for themselves

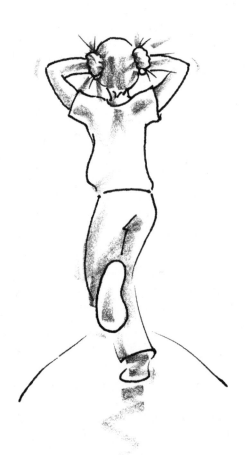

If ....

If ....

If ....

How **good**

could you

stand it ?

The only thing

worse

than

not being in a relationship

is

being in one

you wish you were not

THE MOMENT

I

depreciate

MYSELF

I

ROB OTHERS

I will <u>not</u>

SHOULD

on myself

today

I'll not

intentionally

Should

on

anyone else

today

either

I used to live

the way

I thought I should

NOW

I

Live

the way

I

think

41

If you think I'm selfish
please look again

I really do feel
a lot
of compassion

for you
and
for me

Thank you

for making room

in your life

for me

If we pour
our best
positive energy
into the world

the world
will work better

If others

have **used** us

it is because

we have

let them

If you

<u>really</u>

value me

you will only want

to add

to my life

THINK

BIG

UNLESS YOU WANT TO

THINK SMALL

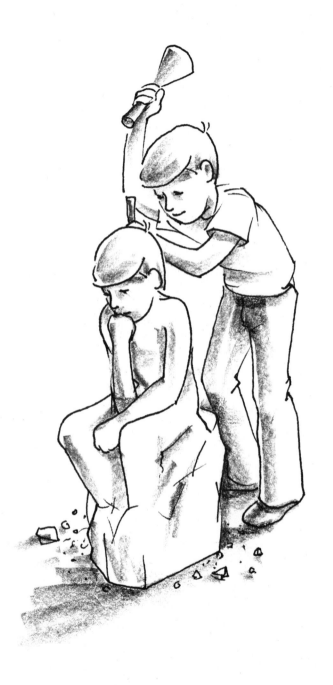

What

you

IMAGINE

can

come

about

Where you

put

your

attention

is

where

you will go

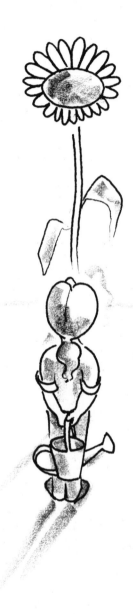

POSITIVE THOUGHTS

AND ACTIONS

BRING

POSITIVE RESULTS

Magic

is

inside

us

MATURE PEOPLE

DON'T

TELL YOU

YOU'RE

IMMATURE

WHEN YOU CRY

Sometimes

I

need

to

be

alone

If I'm too busy

for you

it's because

I have

other priorities

There's nothing
wrong
with you

YOUR

F-A-R-T-H-E-S-T

journey

WILL BE

TO DISCOVER

THE TRUTH

INSIDE YOURSELF

The more someone

IRRITATES me

the more I know

I have something

to learn

about myself

from that person

Until we

think

and

act

out of love – not duty

we will

put ourselves through

all kinds of turmoil

You

were born with

CREATIVE

genius

If you never
take chances

you may be

safe

but

probably bored

and boring

THERE

ARE

NO

GUARANTEES

It's more difficult

to love or respect

those

who have *different*

values and goals

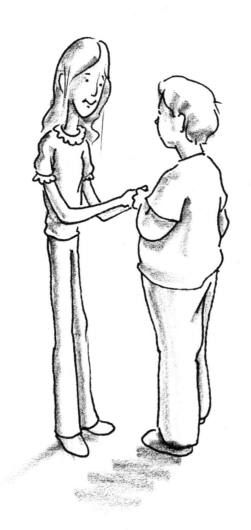

On the inside

we are very much alike

It's on the outside

that we are most

different

If you have not

exposed yourself to

choice

you may wonder

if you are

satisfied

with what you've got

Dream a life

Live

your

dream

It's difficult

to have both

R**I**SK

and

CERTAINTY

At the

same time

There are

positive qualities

in everyone

you

<u>can</u>

find them

It's

Infinitely

more important

to show

how much you care

than show

how much you know

WE

GET

WHAT

WE

WANT

MOST

To those of you

who didn't believe in me:

you may have helped me

more than you or I

realized

at the time

I
appreciate
those
who
believe in me

especially
when I don't

Thank you

for telling me

you loved me

when you did

WE NEED
TO LEARN
TO SAY

"GOOD-BYE"

BEFORE

WE CAN SAY

"Hello"

Barry Trower is a painter and illustrator
whose work has been exhibited in Canada
and abroad. He is currently living and
working in London, Ontario